T0266674

STEPHANIE
MCDYRE JOHNSON

How Can
I Care for
Creation?

CHURCH
PUBLISHING
INCORPORATED

A little
book of
guidance

Church Publishing
19 East 34th Street
New York, NY 10016
www.churchpublishing.org

Cover design by Jennifer Kopec, 2Pug Design
Typeset by Denise Hoff

A record of this book is available from the Library of Congress.

ISBN-13: 9781640652088 (pbk.)
ISBN-13: 9781640652095 (ebook)

Printed in Canada

To my beloved children, Kyra and Robert,
and to all future generations. I hope you know,
in your hearts, that I tried to make a difference
for your sake, God's sake, and all of creation.

Contents

Introduction

I grew up in the Hudson River Valley, in a small farming town about sixty miles north of New York City. When I imagine the Hudson River with its gently sloping hills and meandering riverbed, I feel a deep sense of connectedness to God's earth. The seasons are vivid in the valley, from brightly colored red and orange leaves in the fall, to the mint green buds in the spring, the flourishing vibrancy of the summer growth, to the starkness of the winter snow against the barren trees.

It is here along the Hudson River where I experience a profound sense that God knows me and I know God. In the midst of creation there is but a small separation between heaven and earth; a thin space where the presence of the Divine is palpable.

This knowledge of God's presence in nature is one that many people experience. When I lead talks on creation care, I invite people to reflect on where they most deeply experience God. Most often the response is tied to nature—on the top of a mountain, standing at the side of the ocean, in a quiet forest, or even an urban park. Sometimes these experiences of God in nature are memories that include childhood or family gatherings, a powerful reminder of our interdependent relationship with both people and nature.

My memories of the Hudson River Valley cover decades of my life. As a child I recall being on the Hudson *Clearwater* sloop, an educational experience led by environmental activist and folk musician Pete Seeger. Beginning in the 1960s and continuing until his death in 2014, Seeger was a leading voice in raising awareness of the fragility of the land, water, and air. He engaged people through both his music and environmental educational initiatives.

With his vision, Seeger created an experience of sailing on the *Clearwater* as educators taught both sailors and guests about the ecology and environmental degradation of the river.

Thus my elementary school memories in the 1970s include a field trip on the *Clearwater*, learning about the pollution coming primarily from upstream factories. I would discover later that the pollution included PCBs, chemicals that were destroying fish, particularly the shad that had been running in the Hudson for centuries. But from that short field trip, I retained a searing memory of a polluted river that was essentially dead. Over the years that "educational sail" would come back to me as a stark reminder of the ability humans retain to nearly destroy the environment.

When I began a career as an environmental planner and educator, it became clear to me that local environmental issues could often be addressed by engagement with various community stakeholders. For me, that area of focus was the New York City watershed, which included the areas of upstate New York not far from where I grew up.

More than twenty-five years after my *Clearwater* sloop field trip, I would take my two elementary school–aged children to our local beach on the Hudson River, a waterway earnestly restored to life through the efforts of new laws and local advocacy. We often attended the annual Hudson River Clearwater Festival which marked the resiliency of the waters, the return of healthy fish, and the committed engagement of the communities around the river.

During my years as an environmental professional, I liked to talk about "doing the right thing" for the environment, as my husband and I raised our children in the Hudson River Valley, the backdrop of a thriving, resurrected habitat. Yet some part of me felt a certain lack of conviction that "doing the right thing" was enough of a motivation to continue working toward environmental protection. All too often environmental activists became burned out in their passion, and ecological issues were seen by many as a fringe concern in the face of so many other pressing local and regional issues.

When I entered seminary in 2007, I believed that my career as an environmentalist was over. As I turned my eyes toward priestly ordination in the Episcopal Church and arrived at Berkeley Divinity School at Yale, I began to realize that my sense of calling was not only to ordained ministry, but to a broader ministry of care for creation, or eco-ministry. At Berkeley, as in many other seminaries, programs are offered to educate lay and clergy leaders in the theology, environmental ethics, and biblical interpretation of care of creation. Somehow, with God's guidance, I wound up in a seminary that, along with the Yale Forum on Religion and Ecology based in the Yale School of Forestry and Environmental Studies, helped me make the connection between my lifelong love of God and my care for the earth.

Taking classes and talking to seminarians and professors who were also deeply committed to this, I was inspired to finally consider that taking care of the environment was not a matter of "doing the right thing," but rather a matter of loving and caring for all that God loves. Through the grace of God, my career as an environmentalist and my calling to ordained ministry became one.

This little book is your invitation into a similar journey of exploration. Perhaps you are a committed environmentalist who sees your faith life separately like I did. Perhaps you are a concerned environmental activist who is burned out on feeling a sense of responsibility for the work and are seeking God's presence in the ministry. Perhaps you are in despair and face a sense of hopelessness over the relentless news of climate change because of its current and future impacts on the earth. Perhaps you sense the wonder and joy of God in creation and long to celebrate today, while protecting it for future generations. Or maybe you experience all these things.

Wherever you are on your spiritual journey, I hope this book offers you a sense of possibility and boundless hope for all of God's creation.

1 ▪ *What Does the Bible Say?*

Since ancient times, people understood that human connection to the land, creatures, plants, water, and sky was central to their relationship with God. Scripture taught that God was the Creator and that the abundance of God's creation was to be celebrated, preserved, and protected for mutual flourishing. In the past few centuries, the idea of mutuality has been lost as humans have placed themselves in the center of creation by controlling, managing, and destroying natural resources for their own good.

Here we will explore the connection between all creation and God in the Hebrew Scripture and New Testament. Through this very brief review of some key biblical passages, we can better appreciate that harmony with and care of creation is not a new theological trend, but rather a core understanding of our faith tradition.

God as Creator

Most civilizations have a creation story. These stories help give a sense of a divine presence in the activity of creation, explaining the reason for human existence and the natural world. While countless books and academic papers have explored the biblical understanding of creation and humankind, space does not permit a deep review of this issue. However, as an introduction, a closer read of Genesis is important from an eco-theology perspective.

The story of creation in the Book of Genesis is a reminder that God created out of nothingness. Over the course of the six days of God's time, creation exploded into being with sky, water, air, land, and all sorts of animals including creepy-crawly things and birds in the sky. This imagery recognizes a powerful sense of how God's presence stood at the center of creation.

Recall that humans were made in the image of God on the sixth day of creation, directed to subdue the earth, and given dominion over all creation. For most ancient peoples , the idea of humans subduing and having dominion over nature was never seen as a possibility. The reality was, for most of human existence, that people were at the total mercy of nature. Droughts or floods could mean total devastation for communities totally reliant on small or family agriculture. Humans in biblical time strived to live in harmony with the natural world and recognized that in many ways they were at the leniency of nature and God's mercy. To kill animals for survival was understood; however, the ability to subdue and completely destroy creation or the land itself was never an ancient understanding.

From an eco-theology reading, biblical scholars suggest that dominion can be seen as if a benevolent royal oversees a kingdom. To ensure that the entire kingdom or community flourishes, each part of creation should also flourish, rather than be destroyed or abused.

Equally important is that on each day that God created, God saw that everything was good. All creatures were equally blessed in God's plan. Humankind was invited to be stewards and caretakers of all the bounty of God's creation, not the center of it, which time and technology has changed.

The second creation story begins in Genesis 2–4a: After God created the heavens and the earth, God created man out of dust from the ground. Humankind has its very origin from the land, as the work of creation continued with the Creator as the gardener in Genesis 2:8–9:

And the Lord God planted a garden in Eden, in the east; and there he put the man whom he had formed. Out of the ground the Lord God made to grow every tree that is pleasant to the sight and good for food, the tree of life also in the midst of the garden, and the tree of the knowledge of good and evil.

We read that God intends man "to till . . . and keep" the land (Genesis 2:15). Humans are meant to cultivate the land by God's direction. Interestingly, the word "keep" in Hebrew is *shamar,* which can also mean guard. Humans are responsible for ensuring that the land is protected for its purpose as a source of abundance for all creatures. Flourishing, thriving land will provide goodness and crops for humans while equally ensuring that the land too prospers for God's purpose.

Psalm 104 further elaborates God's role as Creator. Beginning at the first and repeated at the last verse, God is celebrated and thanked for the very act of creation:

Bless the Lord, O my soul.
O Lord my God, you are very great.

From there, echoing the creation themes in Genesis, the psalmist reveals God stretches out the heavens like a tent (v. 2), setting the earth on its foundation (v. 5) and giving boundaries to the flowing of the waters. We are then reminded that God created the day and night and the seasons:

You have made the moon to mark the seasons;
    the sun knows its time for setting.

You make darkness, and it is night,
    when all the animals of the forest come creeping out.
The young lions roar for their prey,
    seeking their food from God (v. 19–21)

As a reminder of the power of God's creative forces in the Book of Job, God appears to Job to question whether he really appreciates the majesty and strength of God as creator. After all the wondering and struggles Job faces in fear, uncertainty, sickness, and loss, God appears to Job to remind him about how Job is but a small part of God's vast and immeasurable creation. God reminds Job that in his limited human understanding he can barely appreciate the immensity of God's creative efforts:

> Then the Lord answered Job out of the whirlwind: Who is this that darkens counsel by words without knowledge? Gird up your loins like a man, I will question you, and you shall declare to me. Where were you when I laid the foundation of the earth? Tell me, if you have understanding. Who determined its measurements—surely you know! Or who stretched the line upon it? On what were its bases sunk, or who laid its cornerstone when the morning stars sang together . . . ? —Job 38:1–7

Throughout the Hebrew Scripture, there are numerous references that the land itself is deserving of respect, for it is from God. Leviticus 25:4 states:

> . . . but in the seventh year there shall be a sabbath of complete rest for the land, a sabbath for the Lord; you shall not sow your field or prune your vineyard.

The practical reason for resting the land is that it will be more productive. However, when placed in the context of the Lord's sabbath it is a sign that all creation is to be treated with value and respect as part of God's creation.

Creation Celebrates and Mourns

Through Hebrew Scripture we also learn that human attributes, such as the ability to praise and to mourn, are shared by other parts of creation. Creation is seen as having equality with humans with the similar capacity to recognize the Creator. The prophet Jeremiah reminds us that the land itself will grieve when it and humankind are mistreated, and when the land is unwell other parts of creation suffer also.

> How long will the land mourn, and the grass of every
> field wither? —Jeremiah 12:4

The prophet Hosea reminds the Israelites that separation from God and God's expectations will cause not only the land but also the rest of creation to grieve. Again, we are reminded that the relationships between land, nature, and people are deeply intertwined. When one aspect of the creation is degraded, another part suffers.

> Therefore the land mourns, and all who live in it languish;
> together with the wild animals and the birds of the air,
> even the fish of the sea are perishing. —Hosea 4:3

Scripture tells us that while not only can the land mourn, all creation can be in harmony rejoicing in God's abundance as an interconnected, dependent community. When all is well with nature and balance is achieved with the blessing of God, nature responds like humankind with joy, happiness, and even singing:

> The pastures of the wilderness overflow,
>> the hills gird themselves with joy,
> the meadows clothe themselves with flocks,
>> the valleys deck themselves with grain,
>> they shout and sing together for joy.
>>> —Psalm 65:12–13

Not only does the land rejoice but the entire cosmos celebrates God:

> Let the heavens be glad, and let the earth rejoice;
>> let the sea roar, and all that fills it;
>> let the field exult, and everything in it.
> Then shall all the trees of the forest sing for joy . . . .
>>> —Psalm 96:11–12

The New Testament

The New Testament is steeped in reminders of the centrality of nature from agricultural references to reminders that Jesus' ministry was set in various landscapes. In fact the backdrop of many of the gospel stories include numerous stories of Jesus outside in nature. Remember, the very first introduction of Jesus is his birth in a manger, presumably surrounded by animals. The first people to greet Jesus were shepherds who lived out under the sky (Luke 2:8–20).

As Jesus grows into adulthood, we can almost imagine him walking down through the grass and brush alongside the riverbed, wading into the Jordan River as he is immersed in the life-giving water when baptized by John. Looking up to the blue skies, the clouds open up to reveal God. All of nature is present for the baptism of Jesus.

His disciples, all who came to hear him preach and sought healing, met him in fields, mountains, or near the sea. We can almost see Jesus strolling on dusty trails to give the sermon on the plain or, walking beside the vastness of the Sea of Galilee, inviting his disciples to give up their work of fishing to follow him. He rested in the mountains, meeting people at water wells and street corners as he journeyed through villages and towns. Jesus' disciples were in the fields picking grain on the sabbath.

However, the gospel writers not only placed Jesus ministering outside, they also equated Jesus and his ministry with nature. In the imagery of John's gospel, the reader is invited to consider that Jesus is actually part of nature.

> I am the vine, you are the branches. Those who abide in me and I in them bear much fruit, because apart from me you can do nothing. —John 15:5

Jesus is compared to a vine, part of a growing living tree or bush that stretches and bends as it thrives with sun and water. Humans are described as part of the branches that come out from nature, an imaginative sign of our connection to Jesus and to nature.

The parables of Jesus are full of references to nature, farming, vineyards, water, and the land. The intention is clear that the first listeners of the gospel stories understood the relationship humans have with nature. As farmers and fishermen, they knew the cycles of life were dependent on nature. While some lived in urban settings, they still lived close enough to the land to be reliant on good weather for food. Consider the parable of the sower who plants seeds in the field with mixed results; birds take the seeds when they are not buried, rocks prevent some of the soil from being fertile (Luke 8:4–8). In Matthew 13:8 are the seeds used to full fruition:

> Other seeds fell on good soil and brought forth grain, some a hundredfold, some sixty, some thirty.

It's not only the parables that accent the relationship between Christian faith and the natural world. Particularly important from an eco-theological perspective, Jesus urges the disciples to "Go into all the world and proclaim the good news to the whole creation" (Mark 16:15). From these words, we are reminded that the early followers of Jesus understood that the promise of redemption and new life in the gospel message was not only about human renewal, but also about the flourishing and re-creation of all that God creates. In our time, we should also hear this as the promise of the Good News is for all creation, not just humans.

Exploring further in the New Testament, Romans 8:22–23 is often read from an eco-theological perspective:

> We know that the whole creation has been groaning in labor pains until now; and not only the creation, but we ourselves, who have the first fruits of the Spirit, groan inwardly while we wait for adoption, the redemption of our bodies.

In this short passage, eco-theologians suggest that "creation groaning in labor pains" can be seen as the widespread pollution of the earth. We are invited to reflect that all of creation awaited Jesus for the fulfillment of the promise of redemption.

In a remarkable bookend to the opening of the goodness of all created things in Genesis, the Bible concludes with the Revelation to John which reveals God's hope for all creation. John the Divine is given the vision from God of a new Jerusalem where the two rivers join for a world that lives in harmony, where all the world is healed and renewed, with bright flowing clear water, and trees that support and sustain all creation.

> Then the angel showed me the river of the water of life, bright as crystal, flowing from the throne of God and of the Lamb through the middle of the street of the city. On either side of the river is the tree of life with its twelve kinds of fruit, producing its fruit each month; and the leaves are for the healing of the nations.
>
> —Revelation 22:1–2

In this closing chapter of the Bible we are reminded that through the power and majesty of God, the promise of healing and harmony for all creation awaits the entire world. God sits at the throne as abundance shines forth for all the nations.

From this very brief overview of biblical passages, we can begin to appreciate that people in biblical times didn't need an explicit theology of the care of creation. They were deeply connected to the natural world around them, depended on the land and water to survive, and strived to live in harmony with all that God had created. From the powerful creation in Genesis, to the hope of new life for all creation, to the promise of healing in the book of Revelation, creation can thrive and flourish as God intended when harmony is achieved. In our time, for the sake of all God's creation, we are called to retrieve and remember those shared memories from long-ago generations of connection to the world around us.

For Further Reflection:

- Read both accounts of creation: Genesis 1:1–2:3 and Genesis 2:4–24, plus Psalm 104. What are the similarities and differences in the three accounts of creation?
- How do you imagine "creation groaning in labor pains" (Romans 8:22) at the beginning of time as well as today?

2 ▪ *Our Separation from God, Nature, and Each Other*

How did we get so far away from the centuries-old scriptural tradition steeped in nature-based biblical stories? Did we forget that humanity, for most of our existence, relied on and feared nature? Did we somehow forget that message that the Good News of Jesus was about all creation? Did we forget that humans have always counted on one another, and the earth, for survival? In this short chapter, we will briefly explore these questions on our journey to restore and reclaim a right relationship with all God's creation.

Human Separation from God's Creation

Theologians and historians suggest that with the Age of Enlightenment there began a separation between God and creation. In an age when reason was seen as a high value, the stories of creation having human characteristics or humans as an equal partner with all creation were dismissed. As seekers in the Enlightenment, it was believed that the essence of humankind was superior and all knowing. Humans ruled and controlled nature for their own advancement. Thomas Jefferson went so far as to rewrite his Bible to take out all the Jesus miracle stories as they couldn't be proved or based on anything that could be reasoned.

Growing scientific knowledge created a false dichotomy between science and religion, suggesting that science could undermine scriptural and church authority. Ultimately this sensibility pitted religion and science as two different forms of understanding the world, creating uneasy relationships between the church and scientific inquiry. As science began to unearth a deeper understanding of how things were created, the Bible could no longer offer a literal narration of creation.

With the release of Charles Darwin's *On the Origins of Species* in the mid-nineteenth century, an even deeper divide between faith and reason developed. Darwin's book was a treatise on the evolution and development of species with scientific research. The book and other contemporary work undermined the concept of creationism. If science could be used to fully describe how creatures and plants were created and related to each other, what need was there to believe in a God that created and sought harmony? It is this perceived threat to the literal interpretation of the Bible that still divides American Christians, some who do not believe in the scientifically proven theory of evolution.

The Industrial Revolution seemed to exacerbate the growing separation between God and creation. With the movement in the United States toward urban areas, mass migration resulted in people moving away from agrarian lifestyles. No longer did people remember the cycles of the seasons and their dependence on good seeds, abundant rain, and fertile land for harvest. With rapid technological advances, the idea of subduing and imposing dominion over nature seemed all the more possible. Factories spewing forth air, land, and water pollution began to create a consumer-driven society.

A well-received academic paper called the "Historical Roots of Our Ecologic Crisis," written by historian of medieval science and technology Lynn White Jr. in 1967, claimed that the Judeo-Christian belief system leant itself toward dominion and ultimately abuse over creation. White posited that at the heart of the mid-twentieth century environmental problems was a post-Enlightenment worldview that the advancement of humanity took precedent over the rest of creation. The degradation and destruction of the earth was essentially a by-product of the advancement of humanity, ordained by God in giving humanity dominion. While some current academic thought suggests that White's thesis overstated the impact of Judeo-Christian thought on environmental degradation and misuse of resources, his position does offer a provocative position from which to consider humanity's lack of concern for the earth.

With the rise of agri-business and corporate farming, small farms were abandoned and often generations of family connections to the land disappeared. The expansion of international shipping offers (for many people) the year-round availability of vegetables and fruits. There is no longer a need to wait for a particular season for food to be purchased at local supermarkets. Droughts and floods rarely affect Americans' access to produce, unless by prohibitive rising costs.

It's not only our lack of connection to our food sources that has separated us from the cycle of the seasons, but people, particularly in America, have generally become more detached from nature. The term "nature deficit"[1] was developed to reflect that people are no longer spending time outdoors. Children no longer play outdoors on a daily basis as was the norm just a few decades ago. For some the constant desire for technology and screen time takes away opportunities to be out in nature, roaming on trails, walking through the forest, and playing at an urban park. In our frenetic-paced world, the time-aged traditions of sitting on front porches and city stoops to talk or pausing to watch the sunset have become a rarity for many. Particularly in the United States, we have lost connection to the land, air, and water—God's beloved and beautiful creation.

The stories in the Bible once reminded people about God and the connection to the land. Due to our detachment from the land and nature for many of us, these are no longer lived shared experiences; rather, they are seen as events lived by people in a distant culture, leading to a decline in our understanding of our interdependence on the earth.

Environmental Racism and Climate Crisis

As humanity has somehow forgotten its shared connections to each other and the earth, many vulnerable communities and the planet have been deeply and irreparably harmed. Indigenous people, people of color, and the poor were (and are to this day) still more likely to be living in areas with severe environmental degradation. The placement of sewage treatment plants, incinerators, and coal burning plants have been systematically located in areas with minority populations. Unhealthy drinking water and polluted air have been a continued concern for communities of color in urban areas. Environmental racism is a phrase that describes "whether by conscious design or institutional neglect, actions and decisions that result in disproportionate exposure of people of color to environmental hazards and environmental health burdens."[2]

Beginning in 2000 and continuing through 2018, the General Convention called on the Episcopal Church to oppose environmental racism. In 2018, "the church affirms that no community, especially poor communities, those who live closest to the land in subsistence cultures, and members of marginalized ethnic groups, should bear a disproportionate risk of environmental pollution or degradation; and advocates for and supports policies that protect these populations and the sanctity of communities and the livelihood of future generations from the disparate impact of climate change and environmental degradation."[3] The Episcopal Church recognizes that environmental racism is a sin that separates us from God, creation, and all God's beloved people.

Partially because of our separation from creation and lack of concern for the natural order, the entire world now faces a more ominous environmental crisis. Climate change, originally called global warming, is a recognized threat to the world today and for the future. Scientists began calling attention to the phenomenon as early as the 1950s, however, it wasn't until the 1990s that it began to be raised in the public consciousness as a threat to the entire planet. The most recent scientific data from the international community acknowledges the impact of climate change is not only real but will be devastating to countless communities and nations. In 2019, some scientists, organizations, and governments began calling climate change a climate emergency given the urgency of the situation.

As climate change exacerbates, people who live near the water and island nations are and will be severely impacted. The poor and indigenous communities will be the hardest hit without resources to adapt to a changing climate. Changing and unstable weather patterns are causing droughts and floods, destabilizing food production systems and economies. Water scarcity in regions with historically dry conditions will cause unstable political conditions. Species are becoming extinct at rates not seen in millennia. This is further exacerbated by localized pollution causing the loss of biodiversity and habitats. According to the Centers for Disease Control and Prevention, public health impacts from climate change will include increased cases of Lyme disease and malaria, asthma, and cardiovascular disease.[4]

In geologic and biblical time frames, it's only relatively recent history in which humankind has been so separated from God's creation. Yes, during this time many lives improved as food and consumer goods became more available and abundant. These shifts may be seen as a natural progression and advancement for humankind. Scientific reasoning and industrialization were real signs of this progress and can be seen as good use of God's blessings on humans. Humans, as noted in Eucharistic Prayer C, were given "reason, and skill" to share in God's many blessings.[5]

Yet, for all this progress, all creation today and in the future is threatened. While the blessings of progress have benefited many people, climate change now threatens all of God's creation. As people of faith, responding to climate change is a moral and ethical responsibility for all people and creation.

For Further Reflection:

- How do you reconcile the biblical account of creation and the view of evolution, the progression and changing of species over time?
- How often do you spend time outdoors? What is your connection to the land in your daily life through what you eat, where you go, and how you engage with the environment?

- What role do you feel Christians (and the church) should have in advocating for the caring of creation, justice for those impacted by climate change, and governmental policies related to environmental degradation?

3 ▪ *A Short Primer on Eco-Theology*

The gift of theology allows us to envision different ways of experiencing God and God's purpose in our lives and the world around us. At our core as Christians, we understand that right, faithful relationships with God and humans lead us into deeper communion with God. These beliefs hold true for our relationship and responsibility for all the creation. The study of *eco-theology* helps us to consider the connectedness between God, our faith, and the natural order. Explored briefly in this chapter are a range of eco-theological concepts. None of these ideas are mutually exclusive nor must all of them be relevant in our life today. However, at different stages and times in our lives, these concepts may offer ways to grow closer to God, God's creation, and foster our care of creation.

Stewardship and Care of Creation
Humanity has, at least in modern times, chosen progress often with disregard for the impact on nonhumans and heedless of the impact on the earth. This sensibility that humans are the core and central focus of creation is called *anthropomorphism.* As people of faith, we sometimes further this idea of anthropomorphism by viewing our responsibility to nature as stewardship. While the concept of stewardship has an important value suggesting care for future generations, the reality is that stewardship places humans at the center by having power and control over all nature. Equally problematic is that this position can lead to the belief that all of nature is at the disposal of humans so that humans can advance regardless of the impact on the rest of creation. An

eco-theological view suggests rather that *care of creation* provides a deeper and more appropriate position for humans' concern for the natural order. Stewards are managers and overseers, however, as loving caretakers we minister to the rest of creation for the good of all the world.

Environmental Sin

As Christians we understand individual sin and the grace of God's forgiveness. This very same theological understanding can be applied to pollution and degradation of the environment. Pope Francis has stated that human destruction of the environment is a sin. Heedless individual and communal decisions and activities that lead to the devastation of land, water, and air are sinful behaviors. Consider the words of the confession from *Enriching Our Worship 1*, as we are reminded that we seek forgiveness for "evil done on our behalf."[6] These evils could include environmental degradation from factories which provide us with a never ending stream of consumer goods or corporate decisions focusing on profits without regard to environmental impacts. We should also recognize our own individual complicity in environmental sins. When we recognize and confess that our decisions from driving oversized cars, single-use goods, and endless possessions are part of a sinful system of environmental abuse and deterioration, we can begin to step back and reexamine our lifestyles for God's sake.

The Kingdom of God Is Now

Another approach to care of creation invites us to consider how we view God's Kingdom. If we continue to imagine God in heaven and focus our attention solely on eternity, we may lose the need to be present to and attentive to the rest of creation and God's continued creative forces today. After all we may think, why focus on the earth today, when the promise of God is in eternal life? In a similar vein, when we believe that God's Kingdom can only be experienced at the end times, we don't worry about the present time or the condition of the world around us. However, if we view the Kingdom of God as always present, our faith compels us to treat all of God's creation as sacred.[7]

Imagine if every day we looked at the world around us as the Kingdom present here on earth. We would then see air, water, and land pollution as destroying the Kingdom. Picture the Kingdom with flourishing waterways and abundance rather than ravaged by mountaintop removal or polluted rivers. Imagine a world where habitats thrive as all species flourish. Addressing environmental issues becomes an act of care for the present Kingdom that Jesus offers us and all creation.

Renewal of Creation through Hope

As noted in chapter 1, Jesus told his disciples to spread the Good News to all creation. We are reminded that this promise of Good News ensures that through Christ all things become new. As we face the growing threat of climate change, we can sometimes face despair over the enormity of the news. However, Jesus has promised renewal of all creation and that, in the passing of everything old, there will be a new creation (2 Corinthians 5:17). Our faith tells us that with God all things are possible and through our human efforts we can be part of a new, improved creation. This belief is not a rose-colored view of a world made perfect. Rather, with a faith-based understanding, we know that as co-creators of God's creation we can be part of the healing of the earth. Through

God's never-ending presence, we are given hope and assurance as we seek a healthier, cleaner, vibrant creation.

Loving All Our Neighbors

We know that Jesus exhorted us to the greatest commandment "to love our neighbors as ourselves," to treat all people with dignity and respect. In the face of climate change, what if we begin to consider that our neighbors, whom we are commanded to love, might not live anywhere near us? How can we expand our view of neighbors to those who are the most vulnerable to the impacts of climate change and environmental racism? As discussed in chapter 2, indigenous peoples and people of color are under the most threat from rising waters and drought caused by climate change.[8] Making decisions that lessen our carbon footprint, thereby helping in small ways to reduce the impacts of climate change, can further our love of neighbors near and far.

Another way to broaden an understanding of "neighbor" is to recognize that just as God loves all creation, neighbors should include creatures, not just humans. An expanded vision of neighbors allows us to consider how our daily choices affect those who are part of our natural community. For some, this appreciation of neighborly love encourages people to become vegetarians. Others may consider engagement in animal rights as a witness to Jesus's call to love their neighbor.

Eco-Spirituality

Eco-spirituality invites us to consider the reverence and awe that we experience in nature. In moments of stillness and harmony with the natural world, we may feel God mostly deeply. As we gaze at mountains and oceans that have been around for eons, we know that a Divine power has created the majesty before us. In a quiet forest, with old towering trees, we may experience the sense of connectedness to the past and unity with nature. While gardening, digging deep into the soil, we may feel that we are fully grounded to the earth and with the people who have toiled in the soil before us. These times of kinship with all creation are sometimes thought to be the in-breaking of the Spirit, a transcendence when God's presence is palpable. As we experience God's "hand at work in the world around us,"[9] we can harness a sense of gratitude and love. Gratitude for all that God creates encourages us to care for all creation as an act of joy.

Confessing our sins, loving our neighbors, recognizing the present Kingdom of God, living in hope and reverence and believing in redemption, are all expressions of being faithful Christians. Our journey to care more deeply for God's earth is enlivened and nourished when we experience these faithful expressions as the heart of our eco-ministry.

For Further Reflection:

- Do you see yourself as a *steward* or *caretaker* of creation? How and why?
- List some specific ways you can be part of healing the earth.
- Do you believe that environmental destruction is a sin? What are some specific examples in your life?

4 ▪ The Episcopal Church in Caring for Creation

Throughout these times of environmental instability and uncertainty, the Episcopal Church has and continues to be a strong voice of hope and possibility in God's name, leading in the intersection of ecology and faith.

A Short History of What We've Accomplished

In response to the growing ecological threats, the church recognized that worship should begin to reflect a concern and care for the earth. With the 1979 Book of Common Prayer, a new Eucharistic Prayer "C" was written against the backdrop of national environmental activism that recognized "this fragile earth, our island home"[10] while celebrating that the entire cosmos was created by God. Unfortunately, the language of dominion and anthropomorphism was reinforced, as the prayer stated that God had made us rulers of creation, placing us in authority and in the center of creation.

In the mid-1970s the Executive Council of the Episcopal Church formed a Task Force on Energy and the Environment. The work of this task force was reaffirmed by the 66th General Convention in 1979, calling upon "every member of the church to exercise a responsible lifestyle, including energy conservation, family planning, and simpler eating habits." Additionally, "mindful of the earth's limited resources," all agencies of the church were asked "to give priority to that concern in meetings and conferences."[11]

In 1991, at the 70th General Convention, a resolution (A195) was passed that created an Environmental Stewardship Team.[12] The team explored the intersections of environmental degradation, poverty, racism, gender inequality, and environmental refugees. They also organized a liturgy and ecology symposium, supported seminaries in developing theological responses to care of creation and created a curriculum for the entire church titled *One God, One Family, One Earth; Responding to the Gift of God's Creation.* Based on this work, the 1994 General Convention theme was "One God, One Family, One Earth."

In 1993, the Cathedral of St. John the Divine in New York City, with the support of a Trinity Church grant, created the first position for environmental ministry in the Episcopal Church. With the additional support and collaboration with Province I (the seven dioceses in New England) and the Anglican Communion office at the United Nations, the Reverend Jeff Golliher became the Canon for the Environment and Coordinator of the René Dubos Consortium for Sacred Ecology at the cathedral. Canon Golliher was hired to weave together new environmental ministries across different levels and parts of the church. This important step marked a turning point for the Episcopal Church as a leader in the faith-based effort to care for creation. In the following decades, the Episcopal Ecological Network[13] would be created. Dioceses and cathedrals would hire eco-ministers to help guide the conversation around the environment and faith.

In the early 2000s, a renewed public debate in the United States emerged around creationism and intelligent design. In some parts of the country, school districts began to require that creationism be taught alongside evolution, giving equal standing to both positions. In response, the Episcopal Church's Committee on Science, Technology, and Faith wrote the *Catechism of Creation* in 2005.[14]

Using biblical principles, theological understanding, and scientific reasoning, the Catechism offers a concrete defense that science and faith are not incompatible. In fact, the Catechism stated that understanding and recognizing science could lead to a deeper appreciation of God's creation. The Catechism affirms both the centrality of the Bible in understanding God's presence in the world, while equaling affirming evolution as a valid scientific theory. The Catechism describes God's creative forces in this way:

> In this evolving universe, God does not dictate the outcome of nature's activities, but allows the world to become what it is able to become in all of its diversity: one could say that God has a purpose rather than a fixed plan, a goal rather than a blueprint.[15]

The General Convention of 2012 officially memorialized the Catechism of Creation.[16] Through this action, the document was affirmed as a statement of the church and confirmed the interconnection between science and faith.

In 2009 the General Convention of the Episcopal Church memorialized the Genesis Covenant, which was based on a national ecumenical effort to reduce energy use in congregations.[17] The covenant recommended a highly aspirational, aggressive goal of reducing congregational energy use by 50 percent by 2020 in Episcopal churches and all communities of faith. While the goals of the covenant were ambitious, the intention to support congregations in seriously evaluating their energy consumption was well intentioned.

For many congregations, the Genesis Covenant raised awareness of the church's commitment to energy reduction as a faithful act of caring for creation. Primarily in response to the Genesis Covenant, the bishops of Province I created the position of Energy Stewardship Minister[18] in 2010 to help congregations and dioceses consider these goals.

In 2011, the House of Bishops issued its first-ever pastoral teaching on the environment. The House of Bishops' pastoral teaching built on a foundational document written in 2003 by Province I bishops entitled "To Serve Christ in All Creation," which urged engagement by the church to care for creation. The House of Bishops lamented the growing threat of climate change and recognized the historic disregard the church has had for the environmental injustices suffered by the poor and indigenous peoples. The teaching also bemoaned the growing consumer culture that created a society fixated on goods and possessions rather than on spiritual growth. The pastoral teaching urged the church to engage in individual and congregational spiritual practices, which included fasting, sabbath keeping, and communal and individual prayer. It also urged the church:

> . . . to advocate for a "fair, ambitious, and binding" climate treaty, and to work toward climate justice through reducing our own carbon footprint and advocating for those most negatively affected by climate change.[19]

In response to this call for active engagement in international treaties, Bishop Marc Andrus of the Diocese of California has led deputation to the United Nations Conference of Parties on Climate Change[20] as a public witness to the concern the church has for all creation. The House of Bishops' teaching positioned the Episcopal Church as an important voice in connecting spiritual practices and engagement in political processes as central ministries for the care of creation.

Under the leadership of then Presiding Bishop Katharine Jefferts Schori, who holds a PhD in oceanography, the Episcopal Church continued its focus on the care of creation. The Episcopal Church hired a full-time staff person who focused solely on creation care. With the bishop's guidance, in 2013 the church held a four-day summit with the Church of Sweden and the Evangelical Lutheran Church of America to commit to a global effort to respond to the challenges of climate change. A shared statement of intent and mutuality urged the churches to *metanoia*—a return to God's ways of harmony and stability—with creation, while recognizing humans' sinful behavior in polluting the earth.

With the installation of Presiding Bishop Michael Curry in 2015, the Episcopal Church affirmed its commitment to three key areas of ministry—reconciliation, evangelism, and care of creation. The Jesus Movement of the Episcopal Church reclaims the biblical tradition, modeled by Jesus, in inviting all people and creation into God's promise of equity, fullness, and abundance of life. In 2015, based on a resolution from the 78th General Convention, the Advisory Council on the Stewardship of Creation was convened to develop a grant program for local and regional eco-ministries, strengthen networking efforts, and respond to eco-justice concerns around the church. In response to a subsequent resolution in 2018 at General Convention, the Council was again convened for the next three years renamed as the Task Force on the Care of Creation and Environmental Racism.[21] The mandates for the new Task Force reflects a renewed commitment to the intersectionality of justice and the environment building on the work begun in the 1990s.

As the church continued its leadership on the moral and ethical response to climate change, the world began to focus yet again on how to respond. In October 2018, the United Nations' Intergovernmental Panel on Climate Change (IPCC) report[22] found that not only is climate change happening faster than previously thought, but that the consequences will be even deadlier and more expensive than previously confirmed, and the world has only twelve years to cut fossil fuel use in half.[23] In December 2018, at the annual United Nations climate negotiations (COP24), two hundred nations were ready to pass a resolution "welcoming" the report.

While the United States joined with two other countries to block the report, the Episcopal Church's delegation to COP24 responded to the United States administration's decision with a letter endorsing science and rebuking climate denial. The letter from the presiding bishop's representatives urged the official American delegation to fully welcome the scientific findings of the IPCC.[24]

Episcopal Voices and Ministries Today

This short history of the Episcopal Church's engagement in eco-ministry would be incomplete without recognizing some of the current Episcopal theological voices.

University of Virginia Professor Dr. Willis Jenkins, a prominent environmental ethicist and active lay Episcopal leader, has urged the church to consider both its complicity in the deterioration of the earth while recognizing that our traditions offer unique and transformative ways to reclaim our understanding of our relationship with God's creation.[25]

The Reverend Dr. Margaret Bullitt-Jonas, the eco-missioner of the Episcopal Diocese of Western Massachusetts and the United

Church of Christ in the Massachusetts Conference, engages the heart and mind in meditative and spiritual practices that deepen appreciation of God's good earth and encourages hope and perseverance in the face of climate change. Reverend Bullitt-Jonas is also an activist who engages in civil disobedience and public rallies as a sign of public witness against environmental injustices.

Bishop Jeffery Rowthorn and Dr. Anne Rowthorn have been pioneers for decades in hymnody, prayer, and worship by inviting worshippers to fully integrate the worship of God with care for creation. Bishop Rowthorn's hymns encourage a new way of seeing the world around us and connecting to all creation. These resources offer prayers of repentance and reconciliation, while also rejoicing in the splendor and awesomeness of creation.

The Reverend Fletcher Harper founded GreenFaith[26] as an ecumenical and interfaith organization working with congregations to consider how worship and action could lead to transformation in congregational and personal care for the earth. The GreenFaith Fellows program invites lay and clergy leaders to participate in a yearlong program of education, networking, and community engagement. Numerous Episcopal lay and clergy have gone through this program, making a significant mark in their local congregations, dioceses, and regions. More recently, GreenFaith has begun to engage in international efforts around climate change.

In California, the Reverend Sally Bingham founded the national Interfaith Power and Light (IPL)[27] organization to help congregations decrease their energy use as a sign of care for God's earth. Statewide IPL chapters were created across the United States to develop local contextual responses to environmental concerns. This structure of local IPLs has allowed the organization to become a significant influencer in local public discourse on environmental issues, a leader in ecumenical and interfaith creation care efforts, and a leader in congregational eco-ministries.

Dr. Richard Acosta, an Episcopal priest and professor at the University of Colombia in Bogotá, offers an important contribution on the relationship between liberation theology, God, and creation in *Dios, Hombre, Creación: Hacia una Ecoteología Bíblica*.[28] Dr. Acosta gives lectures on the intersection of economic and social impacts of environmental degradation.

Bernadette Demientieff is a native Gwich'in from Fort Yukon, Alaska. She is the executive director of the Gwich'in Steering Committee and serves on the advisory board of Native Movement Alaska.[29] Ms. Demientieff travels all over the world to advocate on behalf of her community and all creation that is impacted by climate change and arctic drilling.

While this list of leading thinkers is in no way complete, and more thought leaders are rapidly emerging, the Episcopal Church is well positioned to continue to engage and support deep theological grounding in the care of creation.

Most critically are the untold and often unrecognized eco-ministries across the Episcopal Church which have flourished for decades and occur daily in congregations, schools, monastic communities, camps and conference centers, and dioceses. Since the very first Earth Day in 1970, these faithful communities have reexamined their communal and individual practices to align themselves with God's creation. Developing their own uniquely contextual response, these communities have shown forth God's love of creation to the world around them. From local environmental advocacy, congregational gardens, worship practices and educational forums, Episcopalians have engaged in these pressing issues with faithfulness, fortitude, and vision. In the following chapters, we will explore how individuals and communities can also embrace meaningful eco-ministries that enliven their faith and relationship to God's good earth to join with countless Episcopalians and people of faith from around the globe.

For Further Reflection:

- Read the Catechism of Creation and/or Genesis Covenant. What portions resonate with you and how might you take on some of the practices set forth in them?
- How can you include the care of creation in your prayers each day?

5 ▪ *What Can One Person Do?*

We all become environmentalists when we feel connected and responsible for the larger universe. It can also be overwhelming to think about climate change and global warming and what can be done from a personal perspective. Again, we can turn to God. In Christian thought and in most faith traditions, the concepts of spiritual disciplines lead to deeper connection to God. When the actions of daily environmental activities are married with spiritual reflection and intentionality, meaningful life-changing spiritual practices can develop. What follows are some basic concepts that show how everyday environmental activities can develop into a spiritual quest and deeper love of God and God's creation.

Fasting

Fasting is an ancient religious practice that has its roots in both penitence and an awareness that denying oneself from a particular activity may bring an alertness to the Holy Spirit. In the Acts of the Apostles, the newly forming Christian community fasted in preparation of making important decisions (13:3 and 14:23). For Episcopalians, the Book of Common Prayer invites us to "observe by special acts of discipline and self-denial"[30] during Lent and all Fridays of the year outside of the Christmas and Easter seasons. The Ash Wednesday service encourages fasting as part of our spiritual discipline.[31] Fasting can be a practice that makes us particularly aware of the needs and health of creation.

The mass production of meat "for our current level of [human] consumption has a detrimental impact on our planet, increasing the greenhouse gas emissions that cause global warming and depleting our scarce natural resources, including water, land and energy."[32] An ethical and moral lens leads some to choose becoming either a vegetarian or vegan. The permanent abstinence from meat or any animal products is experienced as a way of honoring God and all creatures.[33]

For others, joining the Meatless Monday movement provides a way to fast on a regular basis, joining with people from throughout the world. Meatless Monday was an international movement founded in 2003 by Johns Hopkins Bloomberg School of Public Health with the goal of reducing meat consumption by 15 percent. People of faith who are committed to reducing their carbon footprint may choose to go "meatless" on Mondays as a fast for God and the earth.

Fasting, however, is not limited to food. In our consumer-driven society, fasting from buying things that we don't really need can also be a spiritual discipline. Often, we are persuaded by society and media that we must have certain items to feel good about ourselves, the newest technology or the perfect product to compete in a particular lifestyle. Retail therapy is a type of thought process that suggests if "I buy something, even if I don't need it, then I will feel better." This type of thinking sometimes leads to binge shopping or purchasing things just for the momentary sense of happiness. A possible spiritual discipline would be to fast from buying anything except that which is absolutely necessary for a period of time, say a week or month. Or join in the international movement called Buy Nothing Day,[34] held on the Friday after Thanksgiving in the United States—the day otherwise known as Black Friday by shoppers. Instead of shopping, use the time to connect to nature: hike, swim, go boating, or walk your dog with friends and family. Most importantly, by *not* buying things we can have a positive impact on the earth.

Science Alerts note that, "By measuring 'secondary impacts'—the environmental effects of producing the goods and products we buy every day—the researchers say consumers are responsible for more than 60 percent of the world's greenhouse gas emissions, and up to 80 percent of global water use."[35] While some of these impacts come from food production, others comes from consumer goods. Take a moment next time you shop to reflect on whether the items you are buying are something necessary for your lifestyle or something that gives you only temporary joy. If it's not a real necessity, take it out of your online shopping cart or real shopping cart and put it back. Then celebrate your decision as a small, but powerful, witness to God and God's creation. In addition to fasting from shopping, consider purchasing used items from tag sales, charity shops such as Goodwill and Salvation Army, and online sites that resell items. This type of shopping is an ideal way to recycle and reuse items that other people no longer need, while being environmentally friendly.

Sabbath Taking

The spiritual discipline of taking sabbath is described in the first chapter of Genesis, when God rested on the seventh day after creation. Taking time from the busyness of life for sabbath makes us more alert to the world around us. Even a few hours away from technology, without our phones and laptops, can help us breathe deeply into the beauty of God's creation. The Book of Common Prayer offers us a lovely reflection for sabbath taking and a link to creation:

O God, in the course of this busy life, give us times of refreshment and peace; and grant that we may so use our leisure to rebuild our bodies and renew our minds, that our spirits may be opened to the goodness of your creation; through Jesus Christ our Lord. *Amen.*[36]

When we take sabbath time to see, hear, and feel the awesomeness of creation, we can readjust our focus away from careers, accomplishments, and possessions. As we draw away from our human desires and wants, we place ourselves in connection with God and the world around us. When we begin to fully understand our complete connection to the natural order, we can align ourselves with the world around us. Then, just as people are in relationship with each other, we become aware of our relationship with all of nature. In this appreciation and recognition of our complete connectedness with all that God has created, we can begin to know and believe that the earth requires our commitment, care, and love. Building this deep relationship with the earth, like all our human relationships, requires time and intentionality. When we give ourselves sabbath rest out in nature, we are giving ourselves to God and God's creation.

Making Intentional, Faithful Choices to Live Lightly

While limiting consumer purchasing is a good spiritual practice, there are many ways to care for God's earth by conscious environmental decision-making. For food and produce, consider buying organic produce and free-range meats, which decrease the impacts on the land and water. Purchasing organic food poses limited financial strain for some people. However, since organic and free-range foods tend to be more expensive than large-scale produced food it can be cost prohibitive for many people who live on tight budgets.

These options for organic food are almost an impossibility for those who live in food deserts, defined by the US Department of Agriculture as typically impoverished areas devoid of access to healthy fruit and vegetables. Much work is needed to address this disparity of access to healthy food. This is an area where leadership and vision in the Episcopal Church can and does plan an important role by the rapid spread of congregational gardens which support local food pantries and soup kitchens.

Supporting local farmer markets, buying from local vegetable stands or directly from farmers, and picking apples and berries helps us connect to the cycle of the seasons as well as to the farmers who work the land. This type of local shopping helps the environment with a smaller carbon footprint. More benefits can result from these types of consumer decisions; we begin to recognize that the harvest is dependent on regular weather patterns, clean water, nutritious soil, and the willingness of workers to farm the land. As a faithful reflection, we can begin "to love our neighbors as ourselves" when we look the farm workers in the eye to express gratitude for their labor. We build relationships with the people who till the land for us and the land that sustains us all.

For decades, community-supported agriculture (CSA) has allowed people to buy shares into a farmer's crops. While sometimes these shares can be expensive, often if they are divided by a few people, it can be less cost prohibitive. Similar to buying stock in a corporation, a CSA share is dependent on the harvest. In challenging weather, either drought or floods, crops will not flourish and the share will be smaller. In years of abundance, the shares may be bigger than normal. Some CSAs require that share-owners work the land as part of their contribution.

In recent years, countless corporations have begun to market green and organic nonfood items. From cleaning products to personal toiletries, opportunities to buy products that are good and safe for the environment are now available in most supermarkets.

There are many ways for people to choose energy that decreases their carbon footprint and saves money. Energy efficient furnaces and boilers can sometimes be subsidized by local grants and loans. Cars that are energy efficient or hybrid can reduce fossil fuel expenses while greatly reducing carbon emissions. Carpooling, walking, and biking to work and church are meaningful ways to reduce our carbon footprint. Getting out of the car can also give us the chance to meet our neighbors and see the world around us. Building relationships with like-minded environmentalists helps us to see the eyes of Christ in others, while realizing that together we make a difference in caring for the earth.

Choosing renewable energy at home is always a great option. For people who can afford solar panels for their home, consider inviting your clergyperson to come and bless the panels. After all, house blessings are considered to be a regular offering during Epiphany; perhaps blessing solar panels on houses during Easter Season as we celebrate the light of Christ can become the norm in the Episcopal Church.

There are endless ways to live more lightly on God's earth and reduce our carbon footprint through reduced energy consumption, thoughtful shopping, and mindful eating. As we choose these paths of environmental sustainability, seek ways to celebrate these actions as offerings of gratitude to God.

Advocacy for God's Good Earth

In recent decades, the Episcopal Church has lived out the biblical tradition of advocating for justice and equality. This practice of advocacy is not of a partisan nature, but rather a reality that God calls us to help transform society and the world for the good of all. We are particularly reminded by the words of the prophet Micah that seeking justice is a God-given call:

> He has told you, O mortal, what is good;
>   and what does the Lord require of you
> but to do justice, and to love kindness,
>   and to walk humbly with your God? —Micah 6:8

The Episcopal Office of Government Relations (OGR) based in Washington, D.C., is charged with advocating for a range of justice issues, primarily at the national level. The topics for which the OGR advocates and lobbies come from resolutions approved at General Convention. In this way, the entire church has a voice in what the important justice priorities are for the church. Over the years, General Convention has approved numerous resolutions relating to the environment. OGR regularly sends out email notices to Episcopalians on items that are before Congress with directions on how to contact representatives and senators. In the recent past, OGR has advocated for the Arctic Refuge and for climate resiliency. Signing up for regular notices from OGR[37] will allow for engagement on concerns at the national level in a very easy way.

Faith-based advocacy at the local and state levels can have a positive impact for communities that are facing environmental threats from polluted water, deforestation, and air pollution from coal plants and factories. Advocacy can include participating in letter-writing campaigns, leading prayer vigils, joining in local opportunities for public rallies, and direct lobbying of local and state officials. Joining with other faith communities, through clergy groups and interfaith organizations, can amplify the message that protecting vulnerable populations from environmental injustices and protecting the earth is a sacred, shared duty. While this type of advocacy and engagement can be done through a congregation, it also can be done by individuals who are seeking to build relationships in the community and deepen their own faith journey. This type of advocacy ministry can require emotional stamina and clarity of focus for an individual, but partnering with others can be supportive.

Conclusion

In recent decades, choosing to live a green life has become much more of the norm, rather than a fringe lifestyle. Making conscious decisions about food, consumer purchases, and energy use offers opportunities for preserving and protecting the environment. With intentionality of focus, prayer, and awareness of God's earth, these good environmental actions can also become part of a spiritual offering to God. In this way, environmental choices become not a burden or responsibility, but rather a spiritual discipline that draws us nearer to God and God's earth.

A person's individual spirituality of eco-ministry can be a profound journey of building a stronger relationship with God. For many, it leads to helping one's congregation and community move toward an ethos of creation care that is life-giving and nourishing to the whole faith community.

For Further Reflection:

- Which of the spiritual practices in this chapter do you already do? How can you deepen the practice?
- How can you reduce your carbon footprint?
- What new practices are you willing to try? Who might help you in being attentive to keeping a new practice?

6 ▪ *How Can I Green My Congregation?*

A green congregation is a community that intentionally recognizes that care of God's earth is central to their community's core ministry. For the purpose of this chapter, the word "congregation" broadly refers to churches, camps and conference centers, schools, and monastic communities. In considering efforts for a congregation to become green, it's important to ensure that the clergy and lay leadership share the same commitment so that it is a transformative, integral part of a community's faith identity. When a green commitment is articulated and engaged by only a few members, it can have the potential to be seen as a peripheral ministry rather than a central act of the assembly.

As a congregation grows together in care of the earth, the ministry can be sustainable, sustained, and nourishing. For many, this means the formation of green teams. These green teams can have the benefit of identifying specific members who are particularly committed to the new effort while articulating a plan for congregational eco-ministry. The green team should, as much as practical, include key lay and clergy leadership.

Ideally, for a fully integrated effort at greening a congregation, every aspect of a church should have members committed to and aware of care of the earth. For example, the vestry (or governing body) would take into consideration environmental impacts when making decisions for spending or investing money. The Building and Grounds Committee would consider the impact of fertilizers on the land. Hospitality groups would eliminate the use of paper and plastic at events while also seeking more sustainable food choices.

In all practicality, it takes time for this approach to become the ethos of a congregation; with a shared vision, persistence, and critical voices, eco-ministries can become a natural part of a community's ethical and moral value system. There are three main areas of focus for congregational eco-ministry: formation, buildings and grounds, and worship.

Formation

If a congregation is brand new to creation care, it is a good idea to begin with congregation-wide education and formation. Advent and Lent are good intentional times to begin this formation. In the early 2000s, the Church of South Africa established a Season of Creation to be celebrated beginning in September. While not recognized officially by the Episcopal Church, as a liturgical season, some dioceses and congregations follow a Season of Creation from St. Francis Day on October 4 through to the first Sunday of Advent. These congregations use this unofficial season as a focus for their eco-ministry programs.

Some churches have set aside an entire church year to focus on creation care. These congregations arrange for lectures, movie series, and special preachers to educate and form their congregation. Episcopal camps have also used various environmentally based curricula to engage campers and camp leaders, incorporating both green activities and nature-focused worship services.

Linking the early eco-ministry efforts to the liturgical calendar helps as a reminder that this is a faith-based ministry, not a list of environmental tasks to be accomplished. As the liturgical season continues, the congregation becomes more in tune with the rhythm of the natural world even in the starkness of a midwinter program.

Advent or Lent can invite reflection on the shorter days, deep life underground, and the absence of flourishing fauna and flower. As these liturgical seasons of anticipation and waiting, repentance, and reflection move toward Christmas and Easter respectively, the natural world continues to change and shift. Formation programs offered during Eastertide can inspire the concepts of new life, seed and growth, regeneration, and re-creation.

As a way to introduce creation care (or reenergize your church's efforts), offer a mini eco-retreat. This can be for adults or an intergenerational event. It provides an opportunity to connect scripture with your local environment, such as your church property, while providing some spiritual nourishment for all. See page 65 for how to implement such a gathering.

Many faith-based resources are available to assist in this formation, including a range of curricula that invite intergenerational engagement. For those congregations that would like to further explore the important link between science and faith, the Catechism of Creation[38] affirms the Episcopal Church's recognition of the theory of evolution, plus—equally important—upholds the compatibility of faith and science.

To dig further into the relationship between faith and science, also from an Episcopal perspective, Bishop and former physics and astronomy professor Nick Knisely's book, *Lent Is Not Rocket Science*,[39] explores God, creation, and the cosmos. Ideal for individual mediation, it also offers an opportunity for small group discussions.

To Serve and Guard the Earth: God's Creation Story and Our Environmental Concern[40] by Beth Bojarski offers a six-week series that starts appropriately at the beginning with the Book of Genesis.

From a narrative perspective, Nurya Love Parish's *Resurrection Matters*[41] explores why the church and creation depend on resurrection and renewal. The book includes questions at the end of each chapter for reflection and conversation. An equally important book is Ragan and Emily Sutterfield's *Church, Creation, and the Common Good*,[42] which addresses the issues of climate change head-on. Opportunities for youth and adult engagement are included in this landmark book. Finally, Jerry Cappel and I penned *A Life of Grace for the Whole World*,[43] which uses the House of Bishops' pastoral teaching from 2011 and an officially adopted position of the Episcopal Church as the outline for a five-week curriculum.

Film series and book studies on topics relevant to the environment and climate change are helpful tools for encouraging conversation and action. It is a good idea to link these book and film discussions to ethical and moral frameworks through group conversation and reflection. Family movies such as *The Lorax* and *Avatar* can foster conversation about the environment for all ages. Documentaries such as *An Inconvenient Truth* and *An Inconvenient Sequel: Truth to Power* set the stage for discussing the urgency of climate change and the need for activism. A short video presented to the United Nations 2014 Climate Summit by poet and climate activist Kathy Jetnil-Kijiner called *Dear Matafele Peinem*[44] is a compelling witness about climate justice, climate refugees, and hope for the future. (See page 75 for more film and book recommendations.)

For these film and book studies, encourage participants to explore the theological implication of current issues. Does a particular film or book raise issues of justice for certain communities? What are the moral implications of lifestyle decisions to drive a certain car, live in a certain house, or eat certain food? How can a community of faith engage the particular topic presented in a film in their local community? Where does God or spirituality show up in the film?

The Yale Forum on Religion and Ecology has made a film called *Journey of the Universe*[45] with a related curriculum. It is a visually compelling film that explores scientific discovery and the awesomeness of creative forces. While never mentioning God specifically in the film, the movie encourages viewers to consider where the Creator participates in creation. The Forum also provides theological statements and materials on a range of eco-ministries and theologies from all faith-based perspectives. It's a wonderful resource to learn about the level of engagement of many different faith traditions and to gain a sense of the broad range of responses and commitments from around the world.

As previously noted, GreenFaith and Interfaith Power and Light have been providing guidance and support for greening congregations for decades. Based in Seattle, Earth Ministry[46] offers eco-ministry formation classes and workshops for communities of faith in the state of Washington as part of their green congregation program. This type of innovative program allows congregations to get spiritually grounded with faith-based formation which fits their congregational needs.

Buildings and Grounds

Buildings and grounds are an ideal area to focus environmental ministries. For many church members, this type of environmental effort produces visual impacts and financial benefits. Making the connection that improvements to a church's property (building and land) help care for God's creation is a reminder that this is a ministry of the church, not just a cost-saving or practical effort. Informing the congregation as each effort is completed helps to raise awareness, particularly if it is announced as part of the greening of the congregation.

The first step to begin a green building and grounds effort is to conduct a physical audit of the property and a review of utility bills. During the property assessment, the team should be alert to areas where energy reduction can be realized. Historically, churches tend to be large and relatively inefficient users of utilities. The Environmental Protection Agency has an energy stewardship portfolio where utility data can be input to track energy use. *The Energy Star Action Workbook for Congregations*[47] guides a congregation on steps to evaluate and assess opportunities to reduce energy use and be certified as an Energy Star congregation.

Additionally, Interfaith Power and Light's *Cool Congregations*[48] program helps communities of faith evaluate and reduce energy use. They offer an easy-to-use start-up kit that can be implemented by a green team to effectively calculate a congregation's carbon footprint and offer suggestions for change; it can also be used in individual households. Often local utility companies have free or reduced cost energy audits that will evaluate lighting and heating/cooling systems. Utility companies may also offer low- or no-cost loans for the installation of energy efficient appliances and HVAC systems.

The Episcopal Church Building Fund[49] offers low-interest loans for energy efficient and other green initiatives including solar panels and new heating and cooling systems. The minimum loan is $20,000, so a congregation should be prepared for a significant project when applying for the loans.

In 2011, Province I (the seven dioceses of New England) began a campaign called "Turn Off the Lights, for God's Sake." Aimed at fostering a faith-based effort to reduce energy use, the campaign invited congregations to place stickers under light switches to remind people to turn off the lights. These small signs in bathrooms and in hallways are a reminder that even a simple act like turning off a light can be an offering of gratitude to God.[50]

Putting on light sensors that turn off lights automatically are also a good way to reduce energy use. Other simple quick fixes include putting timers and thermostats on heating and cooling systems, and making sure that pilot lights on gas-burning stoves are off.

A relatively easy, meaningful way to make an environmentally ethical statement is to switch electric power providers to a provider that uses primarily renewable solar or wind power. While this may cost the congregation slightly more in utility expenses, it is an important commitment to supporting renewal of the earth. This type of effort is well worth mentioning in church communications to raise awareness that even an act of switching utility providers can be a sign of care of creation.

Particularly in older churches, stained glass windows can prove to be challenging for energy efficiency. Over time drafts can occur between the window and the walls, causing significant energy loss. Some churches have been able to design temporary wooden paned glass storm windows, however this can be a significant investment in time and money. A limited number of window companies do this sort of work.

Sometimes churches that are located in extremely cold climates find the cost of heating a sanctuary prohibitive. They move worship services into a smaller space, like the parish hall, for the winter months. Churches then return to the sanctuary for Easter season. This movement of worship spaces is likely a powerful spiritual journey for the congregation to move from one location in the winter months to returning to re-created life in the sanctuary.

Larger and more significant efforts to switch to renewables are options for churches and communities for faith to consider. While the up-front costs may be significant, cost savings may be realized in the long term by installing solar panels or going geothermal. Loans from sources such as the Episcopal Building Fund or local state-run green funds may help offset initial investments. Again, this type of significant effort and expenditure should be celebrated and announced in church communications and local media. A quick search of the internet can show examples of solar panels placed on church roofs in the shape of a cross, a powerful symbol of the Son and the sun.

Churches can make recycling a regular, visible component of church life. Recycling bins for used Sunday bulletins and office papers can show a concern for the earth. Composting of coffee grounds and other food products are a great way to actually be part of the life cycle. New creation is made when our compostable items turn into lovely life-giving soil for congregational gardens and flower beds. Putting a sign above a compost bin that says "Behold I make all things new" (Rev. 21:5) can be a slightly humorous way to encourage composting.

Many congregations have decided to have green coffee hours. In 2014, the Diocese of Vermont Earth Stewards Committee released *The N.R.S.V. (Nourishing, Renewable, Sustainable, Vivifying) Coffee*

Hour Cookbook. The cookbook outlines various steps for making coffee hour sustainable. Among the recommendations is that reduce, recycle, and reuse be the primary focus. Cut out all Styrofoam™ coffee/tea cups and use ceramic plates and cups, cloth napkins, and cloth tablecloths. Serve organic produce and products purchased from local farmers markets or farm stands. Buy local honey for sweeteners. Again, this effort should be celebrated and announced in all church communications.

Within the past few decades, increased interest in healthier, local food sources has taken hold in many parts of the world that previously relied on large, corporate farm crops. This trend, which is really a return to local farms, has also sparked interest in congregations concerned with providing healthy food options to local food pantries, soup kitchens, and parishioners. As foundational as Adam and Eve's mandate from God to till the soil in Genesis, our connection to God and God's Creation deepens when we get our hands in the dirt and get ourselves outside in the fresh air.

Churches in England have used congregational gardens to build community and end social isolation by creating urban and rural gardens that ask for neighbors' participation. Other gardens in England are designed to provide support for people with learning disabilities, dementia, and mental health concerns.

Further, gardens do not need to be limited to suburban or rural congregations with more land. Small raised beds in-between areas of grass can still grow abundant vegetable or flowers in a tiny area. Potted tomato and herb plants can be placed nearly anywhere outside.

Outside in a garden, all God's people can experience the

wonder and joy of planting and nurturing new life. *Harvesting Abundance*[51] by Brian Sellers-Petersen is a wonderful exploration of congregational gardens around the Episcopal Church.

Also important to recognize is that bee populations are declining around the world, threatening not only the species but impacting the process of pollination by which bees help to sustain the food supply. This decline is caused by increasing pesticide use, habitat loss, and climate change. Many communities of faith have decided that they can offer ways to support the bee population. For churches that have the expertise and space, beehives are an opportunity to provide a place for bees to help return them to a flourishing state. Local cooperative extension offices, 4-H clubs, or local Audubon organizations can help guide a congregation in developing beekeeper programs.

Another way churches can support the bee and bird population is to create pollinator gardens. These types of garden are designed to grow native flowers, which provide abundant nectar and pollen for birds and bees. Use of primarily perennial plants is a great option, as they last for many years and become hardy over a period of time. Many garden shops can help design a pollinator garden, or designs can be found on the internet. Designed from native plants, these types of gardens are not dependent on significant watering, creating an additional benefit to the environment. This kind of eco-ministry can be done by any congregation or faith community with little or no space and few volunteers; pollinator plants can be container gardens on porches and small areas. Every type of effort along these lines helps the flourishing of God's good earth.

Remember! Share the good news of your building and grounds

improvements from energy efficient boilers, new lighting, a pollinator garden, congregational garden produce, and beekeeping in all congregational communications. These activities are cause for celebration and rejoicing for God's good earth and for future generations.

Rituals and Prayers

At the heart of every faith community is our shared time when we worship God. As the community of the faithful gather together to hear the Good News and be nourished in word and sacrament, opportunities abound to share a theology of eco-ministry and creation care. A recent survey of ninety-two Episcopal churches by the Reverend Nathan Empsall affirmed that respondents sought to engage in care of creation through deepened "spirituality and/or prayer or by connecting to God through nature."[52]

The Book of Common Prayer Book offers Eucharistic Prayer C, which reminds us of the "planetary courses" and "our island home." This prayer also reminds us that the vastness of God's creation is not limited to our small planet but the entire cosmos. Written during the 1970s, Eucharistic Prayer C reflects a theology of dominion over creation rather than tending to the world as caretakers. Some clergy, with the approval of their bishops, have chosen to use the word "steward" of creation rather than "ruler" in the phrase, "You have blessed us with reason and skill and made us loving caretakers [rather than rulers] of creation."[53]

Recognizing that the church needed to be reminded of the centrality of creation and the Creator, the Eucharistic Prayers in *Enriching Our Worship 1* highlight God's creating force and the giftedness of that creation. Each of these prayers has nuance, which focuses our thoughts in terms of our calling to be caretakers, the awesomeness of the Divine's power, and the beauty of creation. Eucharistic Prayer 1 reminds us of God's benevolence as a sign of God's never ceasing grace and our own failings in responding to the gift of creation:

> You gave the world into our care that we might be your
> faithful stewards and show forth your bountiful grace.
> But we failed to honor your image in one another and
> in ourselves; we would not see your goodness in the world
> around us; and so we violated your creation . . . .[54]

Eucharistic Prayer 2 goes even further in celebrating the creative forces of God, echoing the words of Genesis and the failings of humankind to walk in the love manifested in creation:

> We praise you and we bless you, holy and gracious God,
> source of life abundant. From before time you made ready
> the creation. Your Spirit moved over the deep and brought
> all things into being: sun, moon, and stars; earth, winds,
> and waters; and every living thing. You made us in your
> image, and taught us to walk in your ways. But we rebelled
> against you, and wandered far away; and yet, as a mother
> cares for her children, you would not forget us.[55]

Finally, Eucharistic Prayer 3 brings together a complete presentation of eco-theology with God's creative forces, hope in God's creation, and nature praising the Divine:

> You laid the foundations of the world and enclosed the
> sea when it burst out from the womb; You brought

forth all creatures of the earth and gave breath to humankind. Wondrous are you, Holy One of Blessing, all you create is a sign of hope for our journey; And so as the morning stars sing your praises we join the heavenly beings and all creation . . . .[56]

As mentioned earlier in this book, an important contribution to theology of creation for the Episcopal Church is the Confession of Sin in *Enriching Our Worship 1*. Recognizing and repenting for the damage done to creation is central to our working to restore right relationships with all creation, creatures, land, sky, and water.

We have denied your goodness in each other, in ourselves, and in the world you have created. We repent of the evil that enslaves us, the evil we have done, and the evil done on our behalf.[57]

When we confess "the evil done on our behalf," we recognize that we are complicit in pollution and environmental degradation because of society's unbridled quest for consumer goods, desire for disposal products, and need for new technology.

Worship is of course not limited to Sunday mornings (or Saturday evenings) in a church. As much as possible, try to hold worship outside—in a park, by the ocean, on the top (or bottom) of a mountain, or on the church's front lawn. There in the midst of the wonder of God's creation, worshippers can sense the power of God's presence and the Good News of healing and new life in Jesus. After all, as noted earlier so many of Jesus's sermons were preached on the seaside, mountains, or the plains. Our willingness to follow Jesus's model shows faithfulness to his witness and in a way draws us closer to our faith ancestors who heard the Good

News while out in the open air. The planning and logistics for holding worship outside must carefully and thoughtfully include all worship leaders. Holding worship outside with a regular schedule (for example, twice during the summer or fall or on particular feast days) provides consistency for the congregation. If done well the first time, outdoor services often give a sense of anticipation and enthusiasm for worshipping God in a new space, yet with familiar liturgies.

Other ways to bring care of creation into worship includes expanding the Prayers of the People. Intercessions can give voice to creatures that have no voice by praying for species that are threatened with extinction or have been in harm's way. Lifting up the concerns of people who have become climate refugees from rising waters, tornadoes, typhoons, and hurricanes reminds us of the vulnerability that humans face as the environment changes. Specific mention of local, regional, and national environmental issues serves to let people know that environmental degradation isn't something that is abstract but happens in their own backyard. Raising our prayers with these concerns is akin to us praying for the homeless and the needy; it is about justice and care.

Encouraging, supporting, and fostering a congregation that hears and is receptive to sermons on eco-theology, climate change, and eco-justice is the charge of both the preachers and the congregation. A Pew Research study from 2015 found that 47 percent of respondents have heard about the environment from their clergy, but it doesn't strongly influence their views on environmental protection.[58] However, in keeping with our baptismal promises to seek justice and respect the dignity of all human beings, preachers can help parishioners recognize that protecting the earth is truly the work of the church when connections are made between creation, racism, poverty, and homelessness. Many good resources have become available to assist preachers in developing sermons that are theologically grounded. Blessed Tomorrow[59] has materials on their website that guide preachers in developing sermons that are focused on climate change. *Creation-Crisis Preaching*[60] by Leah D. Schade offers sermon ideas and theological underpinnings for crafting sermons throughout the year.

Of course, praying for and celebrating creation is not limited to our Sunday worship time. *God's Good Earth: Praise and Prayers for Creation*[61] by Anne and Jeffery Rowthorn offers an array of ways to grow closer to God and the earth. Linking themes of justice, praise, celebration, and lament, the book provides resources for all sorts of church and communal gatherings. Many prayer resources can be found on the internet from various eco-theology organizations previously noted. (Also see Resources for Creation Care on page 75.)

When new gardens are established or harvested or solar panels are installed, this is a wonderful time to bless the bounty of God's earth and rejoice in the shared commitment to stewardship. Join in community to sing and celebrate farms and gardens in Episcopal/Anglican traditions that are celebrated on Rogation days. Additionally, St. Francis Day (October 4) is a good day to not only bless pets but also to celebrate a congregational garden or beehive. Both of these liturgies can be found in the *Book of Occasional Services*.[62]

Some congregations have become regular "prayer hikers." These are opportunities for the congregation to wander through nature, share in prayers, and sometimes celebrate the Eucharist. Holy

Hikes[63] is a ministry led by Episcopalians that is "committed to building Communion between all God's creation." To date, thirteen local affiliate chapters of Holy Hikes have been established around the United States, offering regular hiking opportunities for humans and sometimes even pets. The Holy Hikes website provides support for establishing affiliate chapters while also providing resources to learn more about Holy Hike worship services. In 2019 the Diocese of Central Pennsylvania held a week long hike created to reflect the Camino de Santiago in Spain as a Way of Love path across sections of the Appalachian Trail. Offered as a spiritual practice to deepen love for God and the earth, the pilgrimage invited hikers to grow closer in relationship with all of creation.

Worshiping God does not need to be limited to standing on the ground. In 2017, the dioceses of New England and a newly created organization Kairos Earth[64] offered a forty-day "river pilgrimage" from the headwaters of the Connecticut River beginning in New Hampshire to the Long Island Sound in Essex, Connecticut. Hundreds of pilgrims participated in different points along the pilgrimage to join in worship along the shore or to paddle in prayer for a day, a few days, or even a week. Daily prayer and the celebration of the Eucharist at the beginning and end of pilgrimage nourished and fortified the pilgrims, several of whom participated in the full forty days. Using the themes of the 2017 River Pilgrimage,[65] the Episcopal Church in Connecticut has also offered a similar smaller-scale pilgrimage, and plans are in the works to continue smaller river pilgrimages throughout New England. While planning such an event may seem to be time-consuming, even a few hours out in a canoe, kayak, or sailboat with prayers uplifted and songs of praise sung can draw one closer to God and all that God loves.

Moving Forward

Opportunities and possibilities abound for congregations and all faith communities to celebrate and honor God's creation. As people experience transformative moments of worship in nature and engage in communal actions to live lightly on the earth, they can begin to realize that these are ministries of love, not tasks to be completed. Together they can evolve into a congregation that rejoices in the bounty of the earth, mindful of the immense responsibility and trust they bear for the all creation.

For Further Reflection:

- What steps can you take to help your congregation become green?
- Who can you enlist in your congregation to be "creation care allies" for new initiatives?

A Few Final Thoughts

Caring for and loving God's creation as a ministry can be an act of joy and happiness. Seeking goodness in the natural world around us offers time to experience God's bounty. Yet despair and sadness over climate change, the inaction of communities to face environmental injustices, and the threats of local environmental degradation can loom over these efforts.

Engaging like-minded people who share a passion for loving all that God creates, assures us that we never walk this journey alone. As we look to God for strength and wisdom in protecting creation, our hearts will open to experience God's unending love for us, all that is, and all that will be created.

And as our own eco-faith journey unfolds, we can rest in the knowledge of God's promise for creation found in the words of the Revelation to John 22:1–2:

> Then the angel showed me the river of the water of life, bright as crystal, flowing from the throne of God and of the Lamb through the middle of the street of the city. On either side of the river is the tree of life with its twelve kinds of fruit, producing its fruit each month; and the leaves of the tree are for the healing of the nations.

Through this assurance of healing and renewal, we know that heaven comes down to earth with the promise of new life. Responding to that promise of new life in God is why we care for creation.

A Mini-Retreat for Eco-Ministry

This mini-retreat can be used for a Saturday morning or over the span of several evenings. Ideally, the participants should have some access to the outdoors for time for reflection, though this might not always be possible.

Supplies:
- Bibles (one per participant)
- *The Hymnal 1982* (one per participant)
- newsprint
- markers
- 2 spools of ribbon or yarn
- scissors
- small baskets (one for every 8–10 participants)
- one small basket or bowl
- natural items found in your location such as: small flowers, moss, grass, leaves, shells, nuts, pinecones, sand, pebbles, and soil

Advance Preparation:
1. Fill several small baskets with the natural items you have collected from outside the church or retreat location.
2. Cut one spool of ribbon or yarn into 12" pieces, one per person, and place these in a container such as a bowl or small basket.

Opening:
- Welcome participants and distribute Bibles and hymnals.
- Open with a prayer such as:

  Almighty and everlasting God, you made the universe with all its marvelous order, its atoms, worlds, and galaxies, and the infinite complexity of living creatures: Grant that, as we probe the mysteries of your creation, we may come to know you more truly, and more surely fulfill our role in your eternal purpose; in the name of Jesus Christ our Lord. *Amen.*[66]

- Invite participants to talk about why they have decided to participate in this retreat.

Sing: "Hymn to Joy" (Hymn #376)

Read (together, aloud): Genesis 2:4b–25

Prompts to begin a conversation:
- Discuss words and concepts in the passage that were unfamiliar or unexpected.
- How can "tilling and keeping" (v. 15) the land be interpreted for our current context?
- Why do you think humans were entrusted to name the creatures?

Activity: "Creation Care Basket"
Depending on the size of the group, divide up into groups of 8 or 10 people. Explain that the basket will be passed around and each person should pick out an item from the basket which has

meaning for them. Invite people to sit quietly for a few minutes with that item. After the silence, encourage small group reflection on why that particular item "spoke" to the participant. As the group comes back together for large group reflection, ask if any themes had emerged. Note them on the newsprint. Often these moments of reflection will give way to memories of childhood or family (community), the possibility of new life in seeds and spouts (resurrection and renewal), or the beauty of creation (God's awesomeness in creating all that is).

Read (together, aloud): Psalm 148

Prompts to begin a conversation:
- How does creation praise God?
- Why are there particular species and landscape forms that praise God?
- If creation has the ability to praise God, is it sacred in God's and our eyes?

Activity: Take a Tour
1. If the retreat is held in a church, have pairs of people wander around the sanctuary to identify images of creation. Encourage the participants to take notes of all the images that they see. During the group reflection on this activity, note the comments on newsprint. Discuss why churches have historically used nature images in their sanctuary. Do the images of nature represent God (e.g., dove is the Holy Spirit)? Discuss unexpected images of nature in the church.

or

2. Take a tour of the surrounding property and neighborhood in pairs. Notice the types of vegetation, the terrain, and waterbodies. Notice any pollution or environmental degradation (littering, erosion, waterbodies with oil, etc.). Gather together to discuss the tour, and note on newsprint the following: Are there things that were unexpected? What inspired? What showed forth the beauty of creation? Was there a sense of God in nature?

Read (together, aloud): Romans 8:19–23

Prompts to begin a conversation:
- If the creation is groaning, what are specific examples in your community or context that show environmental degradation and pollution?
- How does the concept that creation is waiting for adoption reflect on the environmental movement or eco-ministry?
- Discuss whether redemption of the bodies is limited to human bodies or all of creation.

Read (together, aloud): Revelation 22:1–2

Prompts to begin a conversation:
- Describe the image of the river.
- Why does the tree of life have importance in this passage?
- How can healing be experienced in leaves or in nature?

Sing: "I Want to Walk as a Child of the Light" (Hymn #490)

Call to Action and Reflection:

1. Invite the group to sit in silence for five minutes reflecting on what has been discussed and explored.

2. Review the themes from the creation care basket and tours listed on the newsprint.

3. Invite participants to consider specific actions they can take as individuals and as a community to care for creation and in gratitude for God's abundance.

4. Write those ideas on newsprint.

5. If it seems appropriate, develop a list of next steps for the group.

6. Ask people to reflect on personal commitments for caring for creation.

Activity: Connected to God, Others, and the Earth

1. Invite everyone to stand in a circle.

2. Pass the ribbon spool around the circle, with each person holding a portion as they pass it to the person next to them so that everyone is connected to the ribbon.

3. Explain that we are all connected to each other and the earth.

4. Take a second roll of ribbon and cut off small pieces, give to each participant, and ask them to take a piece as a reminder of their personal commitment to God's earth.

Suggest they tie it to their keyring, or put in their car visor or on a mirror. Place, as appropriate, the larger ribbon on the altar at a worship service as an offering to God.

Closing:
- *Read together:* Psalm 104
- *Sing:* "All Creatures of Our God and King" (Hymn #400)

Notes

1 Richard Louv introduced the term "Nature-Deficit Disorder" with the publication of *Last Child in the Woods: Saving Our Children from Nature-Deficit Disorder* (Algonquin Books, 2005). He coined the phrase to serve as a description of the human costs of alienation from nature. It is not meant to be a medical diagnosis.

2 http://www.columbia.edu/cu/EJ/definitions.html

3 https://www.vbinder.net/resolutions/A011?house=hd&lang=en (accessed June 6, 2019).

4 https://www.cdc.gov/climateandhealth/effects/default.htm

5 Book of Common Prayer, 370.

6 *Enriching Our Worship 1: Morning and Evening Prayer, The Great Litany, The Holy Eucharist* (New York: The Church Pension Fund, 1998), 56

7 For further exploration of these concepts, see books written by N.T. Wright and Sally McFague in *Resources for Creation Care* on page 76.

8 This is discussed in more depth in chapter 2.

9 Eucharistic Prayer C, Book of Common Prayer, 372.

10 Book of Common Prayer, 369.

11 https://episcopalarchives.org/cgi-bin/ENS/ENSpress_release. pl?pr_number=79268 (accessed June 5, 2019)

12 https://episcopalarchives.org/cgi-bin/acts/acts_search.pl (retrieved July 12, 2019), email from Reverend Jeffery Golliher.

13 https://www.eenonline.org/

14 https://www.episcopalchurch.org/library/article/new-catechism-creation-published-committee-science-technology-and-faith (accessed March 20, 2019) and https://www.episcopalchurch.org/ files/CreationCatechism.pdf

15 *Catechism of Creation*, 12.

16 https://www.episcopalarchives.org/cgi-bin/acts/acts_resolution.
   pl?resolution=2012-A136 (accessed June 5, 2019)

17 https://www.episcopalarchives.org/cgi-bin/acts/acts_search.pl

18 The author, the Reverend Stephanie M. Johnson, was hired for this
   position in 2010.

19 www.episcopalchurch.org/library/pastoral teaching

20 https://www.un.org/en/climatechange/cop24.shtml (accessed May
   21, 2019)

21 The author was co-chair, along with Bishop Marc Andrus, of the
   Advisory Council and is at present the Chair of the Task Force.

22 https://www.nytimes.com/2018/10/07/climate/ipcc-climate-
   report-2040.html (accessed June 1, 2019)

23 https://unfccc.int/process-and-meetings/the-paris-agreement/
   what-is-the-paris-agreement (accessed June 1, 2019)

24 https://episcopalclimatenews.com/2018/12/12/episcopalians-at-u-
   n-climate-conference-condemn-trump-delegations-climate-denial/
   (accessed June 1, 2019)

25 Willis Jenkins, *Ecologies of Grace: Environmental Ethics and
   Christian Theology* (New York: Oxford University Press, 2008).

26 https:// GreenFaith.org/

27 https://www.interfaithpowerandlight.org/

28 Editorial San Pablo y la Universidad Javeriana de Bogotá, 2015.

29 https://www.nativemovement.org

30 Book of Common Prayer, 17.

31 Book of Common Prayer, 265.

32 https://www.meatlessmonday.com/research/

33 See also the Christian Vegetarian Association at christianveg.org

34 http://buynothingday.org

35 https://www.sciencealert.com/consumers-have-a-bigger-
   impact-on-the-environment-than-anything-else-study-finds

36 "For the Good Use of Leisure," Book of Common Prayer, 825.

37 https://www.episcopalchurch.org/OGR/creation-care

38 https://www.episcopalchurch.org/files/CreationCatechism.pdf

39 W. Nicholas Knisely, *Lent Is Not Rocket Science: An Exploration of God, Creation, and the Cosmos* (Cincinnati, OH: Forward Movement, 2013).

40 Beth Bojarksi, *To Serve and Guard the Earth: God's Creation Story and Our Environmental Concern* (Denver, CO: Morehouse Education Resources, 2010). This is a pay-and-download curriculum: https://www.churchpublishing.org/toserveandguardtheearth

41 Nurya Love Parish, *Resurrection Matters: Church Renewal for Creation's Sake* (New York: Church Publishing, 2018).

42 Ragan Sutterfield and Emily Sutterfield, *Church, Creation, and the Common Good* (New York: Church Publishing, 2018).

43 Jerry Cappel and Stephanie M. Johnson, *A Life of Grace for the Whole World: A Study Course on the House of Bishops' Pastoral Teaching on the Environment* (Denver, CO: Morehouse Education Resources, 2017). This curriculum also offers an adult book and youth book.

44 https://jkijiner.wordpress.com/video-poems/

45 http://fore.yale.edu/multimedia/-journey-of-the-universe-and-the-world-religions/ (accessed May 21, 2019)

46 https://earthministry.org/

47 https://www.energystar.gov/buildings/tools-and-resources/energy_star_action_workbook_congregations (accessed May 22, 2019)

48 http://www.coolcongregations.org/

49 https://www.ecbf.org/

50 https://www.episcopalnewsservice.org/2012/10/15/province-1-launches-turn-off-the-lights-for-gods-sake-campaign/

51 Brian Sellers-Petersen, *Harvesting Abundance: Local Initiatives of Food and Faith* (New York: Church Publishing, 2017).

52 Survey done by Nathan Empsall as a project of his Yale Divinity School thesis (unpublished) 2019.

53 Book of Common Prayer, 370.

54 *Enriching Our Worship 1: Morning and Evening Prayer, The Great Litany, The Holy Eucharist* (New York: The Church Pension Fund, 1998), 58.

55 Ibid., 60.

56 Ibid., 63.

57 Ibid., 56.

58 https://www.pewresearch.org/science/2015/10/22/religion-and-views-on-climate-and-energy-issues/

59 https://blessedtomorrow.org/

60 Leah D. Schade, *Creation-Crisis Preaching: Ecology, Theology, and the Pulpit* (St. Louis, MO: Chalice Press, 2015).

61 Anne Rowthorn and Jeffery Rowthorn, *God's Good Earth: Praise and Prayer for Creation* (Collegeville, MN: Liturgical Press, 2018).

62 *Book of Occasional Services 2003* (New York: Church Pension Group, 2000).

63 https://holyhikes.org/

64 https://kairosearth.org/

65 https://kairosearth.org/river/

66 "For Knowledge of God's Creation," Book of Common Prayer, 827.

Resources for Creation Care

Print or Downloadable

Richard Acosta. *Dios, Hombre, Creación: Hacia una Ecoteología Bíblica* (San Pablo, Colombia: La Universidad Javeriana de Bogotá, 2015).

Jim Antal. *Climate Change, Climate Church: How People of Faith Must Work for Change* (Lanham, MD: Rowman and Littlefield, 2018).

Beth Bojarski. *To Serve and Guard the Earth: God's Creation Story and Our Environmental Concern* (Denver, CO: Morehouse Education Resources, 2010). This is a pay-and-download curriculum: https://www.churchpublishing.org/toserveandguardtheearth

Book of Occasional Services 2003 (New York: Church Pension Group, 2000).

Jerry Cappel and Stephanie M. Johnson. *A Life of Grace for the Whole World: A Study Course on the House of Bishops' Pastoral Teaching on the Environment* (Denver, CO: Morehouse Education Resources, 2017).

A Catechism of Creation, https://www.episcopalchurch.org/library/document/catechism-creation

The Energy Star Action Workbook for Congregations, https://www.energystar.gov/buildings/tools-and-resources/energy_star_action_workbook_congregations

Enriching Our Worship 1: Morning and Evening Prayer, The Great Litany, The Holy Eucharist (New York: The Church Pension Fund, 1998).

The Green Bible, NRSV (New York: HarperCollins, 2010). Also available from Zondervan and at www.greenletterbible.com.

House of Bishops Pastoral Teaching on the Environment, September 2011, https://www.episcopalchurch.org

Willis Jenkins. *Ecologies of Grace: Environmental Ethics and Christian Theology* (New York: Oxford University Press, 2008).

W. Nicholas Knisely. *Lent Is Not Rocket Science: An Exploration of God, Creation, and the Cosmos* (Cincinnati, OH: Forward Movement, 2013).

Richard Louv. *Last Child in the Woods: Saving Our Children from Nature-Deficit Disorder* (Chapel Hill, NC: Algonquin Books, 2005).

Mallory McDuff. *Sacred Acts: How Churches are Working to Protect Earth's Climate* (Gabriola Island, B.C.: New Society Publishers, 2012).

Sallie McFague. *A New Climate for Theology: God, the World, and Global Warming* (Minneapolis, MN: Fortress Press, 2008).

_____. *The Body of God: An Ecological Theology* (Minneapolis, MN: Augsburg Fortress, 1993).

The N.R.S.V. Coffee Hour Cookbook (plus signage for downloading), https://diovermont.org/2014/11/16/the-n-r-s-v-coffee-hour-cookbook/

Nurya Love Parish. *Resurrection Matters: Church Renewal for Creation's Sake* (New York: Church Publishing, 2018).

Anne Rowthorn and Jeffery Rowthorn. *God's Good Earth: Praise and Prayer for Creation* (Collegeville, MN: Liturgical Press, 2018).

Brian Sellers-Peterson. *Harvesting Abundance: Local Initiatives of Food and Faith* (New York: Church Publishing, 2017).

Leah D. Schade. *Creation-Crisis Preaching: Ecology, Theology, and the Pulpit* (St. Louis, MO: Chalice Press, 2015).

Ragan Sutterfield and Emily Sutterfield. *Church, Creation, and the Common Good* (New York: Church Publishing, 2018).

N.T. Wright. *Surprised by Hope: Rethinking Heaven, the Resurrection, and the Mission of the Church* (New York: HarperOne, 2008).

Films

An Inconvenient Truth (2006), https://www.imdb.com/title/tt0497116/ and https://www.participantmedia.com/film/inconvenient-truth

An Inconvenient Truth Sequel: Truth to Power (2017), https://www.imdb.com/title/tt6322922/ and aninconvenientsequel.com/

Avatar (2009), https://www.imdb.com/title/tt0499549/ and www.avatarmovie.com

Dear Matafele Peinem by Kathy Jetnil-Kijiner, https://jkijiner.wordpress.com/video-poems/

The Lorax (2012), https://www.imdb.com/title/tt1482459/

Journey of the Universe and the World Religions, http://fore.yale.edu/multimedia/-journey-of-the-universe-and-the-world-religions/

Organizations and Websites

Blessed Tomorrow, blessedtomorrow.org

Buy Nothing Day, buynothingday.org

Christian Vegetarian Association, Christianveg.org

Cool Congregations, coolcongregations.org

Earth Ministry, earthministry.org

Episcopal Church Building Fund, ecbf.org

Episcopal Ecological Network, eenonline.org

The Episcopal Church's Care of Creation, episcopalchurch.org/creation-care

GreenFaith, GreenFaith.org

Holy Hikes, holyhikes.org

Interfaith Power and Light, interfaithpowerandlight.org

Kairos Earth, kairosearth.org

Meatless Monday, https://www.meatlessmonday.com/research/

Office of Government Relations of the Episcopal Church (Creation Care advocacy), episcopalchurch.org/OGR/creation-care

Yale Forum on Religion and Ecology, fore.yale.edu